# RAG RUGS
## OLD INTO NEW
*Book 3*

by
Debbie Siniska

# D·H·G·M·B

First published in Great Britain 2010
by D.H.G.M.Ball
Glyndale, St.Mary's Lane
Ticehurst, East Sussex
England, TN5 7AX

*For my mum, Hattie Bydawell*

# Contents

Cover images:   front: Swimmer   back: Pink Sun Banner, image courtesy of Victoria Hughes

# Projects

In this book, the third in the series, I hope to encourage you to experiment with different fabrics and a range of techniques. Projects include reverse hooky (Flotsam Wall Panel) and the hand stitched Penny Patch Rug, a Braided Utility Mat from long strips of wide cut fabric, and a Celebratory Banner that has a shaped edge and is made using a shuttle hook.

In the Flower Bag project I have used nylon net, silk and wool together to encourage you to be a bit more adventurous.

This book also looks at some different edging techniques, including complex shaped edges and we will look at some ideas for embellishing your work with beads, buttons and tassels.

The following projects will help you to gain confidence and develop your techniques further.
All techniques are explained in book two and information about tools and fabrics are in book one.

# Child's Bedside Mat

## Hooky mat with shell or flag edges

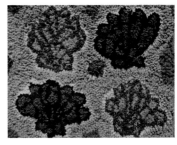

Every child loves a space in the house to call their own and the best place for a little rug especially for them is beside their bed. Use your child's imagination and maybe get them to draw you something for inspiration. Perhaps they have an old woolly or tee shirt that they have grown out of, that could be used to make a memory mat for them!

# You will need

- 10oz hessian no smaller than 35" x 20" (89cm x 21cm)  to give a finished rug size of 30" x 15" (76cm x 38cm)
- Design (your child's or my design)
- Recycled fine-knit woollies, tee shirts, or any stretch fabric in bold colours (and any favourite old /worn out piece of clothing that no longer fits your child)
- Woollen blanket, corduroy or strong cotton fabric for backing, and shell edges
- Rug Hook
- Rug Frame
- Scissors
- Newspaper flag/shell templates (allow for ⅜" (1cm) hem and 1" (3cm) at bottom edge)
- Chalk, magic marker and meter stick
- Strong thread, sewing thread, pins and needle
- Sewing machine optional

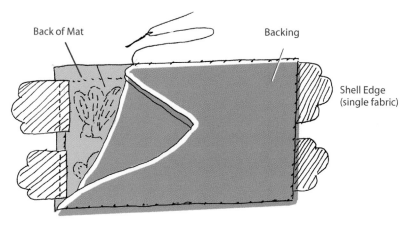

Back of Mat

Backing

Shell Edge
(single fabric)

**Attaching shell/flag edges and backing**

# How to do it

1. Set up your rug frame. Mark out the edges of your mat and trace out your design, first with chalk, then when you are happy with the design, use your magic marker.

2. Prepare your textiles and begin to work the pile (see page 21 book 1 for details on cutting up your fabric and page 9 book 2 for details on hooking).

3. Once you have worked the entire surface of your rug, cut your hessian down around the edge to allow for 3" (8cm) turning and sew down on the wrong side.

4. Lay out your backing material. Cut a piece the exact size of the rug, and lay to one side. There is no need for turning a hem as blanket does not fray.

5. To make the shell edges, first make a scaled-up template of shapes the size you want from newspaper, then draw up scallop shapes and cut out several of these onto a non-fraying fabric such as wool blanket.

6

6 Flag edge – Mark out your flag shapes onto your selected fabrics - cut out two of each. Make enough to go around the edge of your mat if you want to. With right sides facing, sew two pieces together. Stitch a ⅜" (1cm) seam, leaving the bottom edge open for turning inside out.

7 Turn each shape inside out, so the seams are hidden and pinch the edges flat (or use an iron).

8 Place your mat face down, and position the shapes along the edges to see how they work – pin then stitch them firmly into place to inlay 1¼" (3cm) approximately on the wrong side.

9 Now overlay your backing - pin the edges to match the edge of the mat, leaving the flag/shell edges jutting out.

10 Stitch your backing into place, taking care at the same time to properly stitch through the edging you have attached. You can use a blanket stitch or oversew stitch for the backing, and running stitch for the shell edge (see page 17 in book 2).

11 Have a fun ceremony in your kids room for the 'Laying Out' of their beautiful mat !

*Tip:* *You can make a mat larger by incorporating a flag edge when stitching on your backing. If you choose non-fraying fabric such as blanket, you won't have to worry about the edges unravelling. This will protect the edges of your rug a bit more against wear and tear.*

**Right: Flag edge on a braided bench runner**

# Celebratory Banner with shaped edges

## Using the shuttle hook or rug hook

Having a tactile piece of textile art on your wall will cheer up a large empty space and block out drafts if placed above a doorway or over a window. Be adventurous and create something wonderful and celebratory for a space in your home.

# You will need

- 10 oz hessian
  3'4" (1metre) x 5' (1½metre)
- Your design, or the
  one illustrated
- Recycled textiles for
  working the banner and
  for backing
- Shuttle hook or rug hook
- Upright frame
- Cotton string
- Metre stick
- Chalk, old washing up brush, magic marker
- Scissors, pins, needle and carpet thread or strong thread
- Small amount of PVA

# How to do it

1  Attach hessian to the upright frame or the frame you have chosen to stretch
   your hessian onto (see page 18, book one).

2  Using a magic marker, mark the outer edge of your banner, then grid up and
   transfer your design (see page 28 book one).

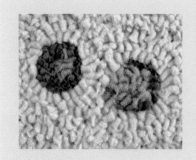

**Tip:** *Try tracing your stitches around key elements of your design to produce a halo effect, to visually draw attention to the focus of the work.*

*In mosaic these lines are called 'Opus Vermiculatum', or worm-like lines tracing out a pattern or design.*

3 Select and prepare your textiles and begin to work the pile with your shuttle hook or rug hook (see pages 12 and 9 in book two).

4 When you have worked the entire surface, remove from the frame and cut down the excess hessian, to leave a suitable width turning of about 3" (8cm).

5 If you have chosen to make a shaped edge, snip into the turning to leave ¼" (½cm), then carefully apply a PVA solution to fold over and secure these fibres – this will prevent fraying at a vulnerable point. Turn down, pin and sew the rest of the hem turnings with strong thread.

6 When you are satisfied with your turnings, you can sew a backing onto your banner, taking care at the curved/pointed edge and attach cuffs for hanging (see page 18 in book 2).

7 Hang your beautiful banner on the wall.

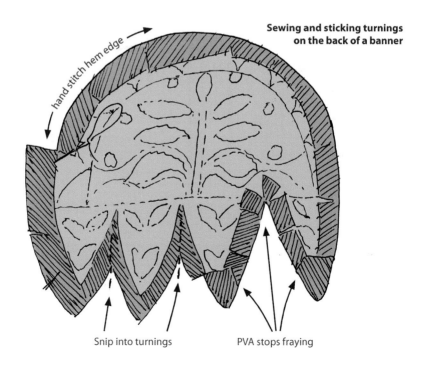

hand stitch hem edge

**Sewing and sticking turnings on the back of a banner**

Snip into turnings          PVA stops fraying

Clipping the pile. On a hooked mat, if you make sure that the end of each strip is pushed through to the front, you can clip them off level with the pile.

# Embellished Flotsam Wall Panel

Using reverse hooking

I have been inspired by the interesting shapes of dried seed heads like fennel and other umbelliferous plants. When they dry out they become truly sculptural. Bring the hedgerow into your home with these tactile wall panels in soft colours, and simplified traced patterns, made clearer by using reverse hooking. Find tiny mother of pearl buttons or beads to decorate your work for added interest, and sew on some tassels - because you can!

## You will need

- 8" square (21cm) cardboard template
- 10oz hessian enough to fit your hoop - use your own inspiration for a design, or use the one illustrated
- Circular embroidery hoop 12" (30½cm)
- Recycled textiles, cut into strips including some dark browns
- Dyed blanket material for the backing
- Rug hook
- Scissors
- Chalk, old washing up brush/Magic marker
- Extra long needle, pins and sewing thread

+ Pretty buttons and other findings for embellishment (optional)
+ Thin garden cane
+ One or two tassels (see page 14, book two)

# How to do it

**Creating a hanging cuff
as part of the backing fabric**

1 Using cardboard template, mark out the square onto the hessian.

2 Now mark out your 'seed head' design inside the square.

3 Press the hessian into the embroidery hoop frame.

4 Cut up your chosen fabrics (see page 21, book 1).

5 Choose a dark brown fabric to trace out your stems and seed heads and begin to hook these definition lines using your rug hook – the back of your hooked stitches will be the 'right side' - this is reverse hooking.

overlapped edge folds
down to form cuff.

Stitch edge down.

6 Work the rest of the square using soft muted colours, with some brighter definition lines.

7 Take your work out of the hoop and turn down the edges. The hooked pile that is normally the front, will be on the back, so your turned edge will be stitched through the hooked pile.

8 Cut blanket doesn't fray so you can sew this directly to the back of your square, without having to turn the hem under. Cut a piece that will fit your work with an extra 4" (11cm) at the top to fold back over onto the backing – this will form the cuff for hanging your panel.

9 Pin and stitch your backing in place, then fold the overlapped edge down, and stitch this in place along the edge only, leaving an opening at either end - see diagram on page 13.

10 Make up two tassels (see page 14, book two).

11 Embellish your work with tiny buttons or beads if you want to, stitching the tassels at the bottom edge last of all.

12 Cut a length of garden cane, to be approximately 11" (28cm) long , to slide through the turned down cuff at the back of your little panel.

13 Hang your little panel along with others you have made for a series.

Oxe-Eye Daisy Cushion

14

Green Man Rug

Rug for Harry Post

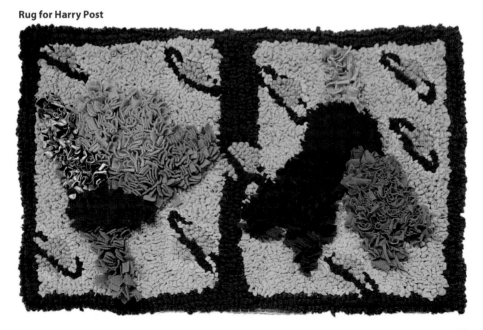

# Braided Utility Mat

Working with plaited strips

You don't need any tools to make this braided (plaited) mat, just a needle and thread! So get hunting and find yourself some bright fabrics to roll, braid and coil into a wonderful weave, to create your own useful and soft mat to stand on whilst washing up. I have used vintage wool blankets for this project, but you could make this mat in cotton fabrics to use as a bath mat. Select fabrics of similar weight for even braiding.

# You will need

+ Woollen blankets or medium weight cotton fabrics (old duvet covers/ cotton sheets) for plaiting and for backing
+ Scissors and tape measure
+ Pins needle and neutral colour strong thread
+ Large safety pin or kilt pin

# How to do it

1 Cut or rip your strips of fabric to be about 3" (8cm) wide. If you are using bed covers, these will give you very long strips to work with. To join strips together, sew a short diagonal seam, which will be invisible when worked in with your braiding (see diagram on page 18). You can do this as you go along, and hand stitch your lengths, changing colour when you want to.

2 Lay out three strips into a 'T' shape and roll the raw edges under then stitch them in place.

3 Safety pin these to a sofa or chair back, then begin to plait.

4 Bring the right hand strip over the central one, then bring the left hand strip over the new central one and continue in this manner, carefully turning your edges under as

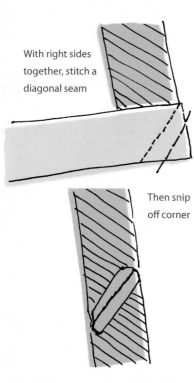

With right sides together, stitch a diagonal seam

Then snip off corner

**joining next strip on for braiding**

you plait. Try to ease your plaited strips round evenly, without pulling them too tightly.

5 When it is time to join a new strip, secure the ends with a pin so it doesn't unravel, leaving a short length un-plaited to make the join.

6 For an oval rug 30" (76cm) x 23" (58cm) fold your central 'coil' over by 10" (26cm) and carefully oversew these butted up edges together at the back.

7 Continue plaiting and coiling your fabric strips, taking care on the curve by easing the strips back against the stitched core, rather than to pull them forward. Your mat will not lie flat if it is coiled too tightly.

8 When your mat measures approximately 30" (76cm) in length, you can bring your slightly narrower cut strips into a tapered point, and stitch them to lie slightly under the outside edge.

9 Lay your mat face down onto your backing material, and cut to size, allowing enough for a 2" (5cm) turning or cut exact if using standard blanket material or a similar non-fraying fabric.

*Tip: As an alternative to a round or oval coil, lay out straight lengths of plaited strips, and stitch the butted up edges together, securing the top edges with a widthways line of stitching. (see bench runner on page 7).*

10 Now with wrong sides together, pin the backing material in place and oversew all the way round (see page 17 book two).

11 To secure your plaited strips, and the backing fabric, work some lines of long running stitches across the back.

**Asparagus Rug**

19

# Welcome Mat

Proggy mat with no-stitch hem

A well placed doormat will be seen by all visitors to your home. It will take lots of traffic so choose durable textiles, and at the same time make it a thing of beauty that will welcome everyone. I used woollen blankets for this project. This mat has a 'no stitch hem'.

# You will need

+ Jute grain sack or 10 oz hessian enough for 30" x 15" (76cm x 38cm) with turnings

- Recycled textiles, perhaps sweatshirts, corduroy, blanket material
- Bodger
- Scissors
- Chalk, old washing up brush/Magic marker
- Metre stick

# How to do it

1 Mark out the perimeter edge of your rug to be 30" x 15" (76 x 38cm) onto your hessian, using a magic marker and metre stick.

2 If you are using a grain sack, cut hessian down to size, allowing a 3-4" (8-11cm) turned in hem.

3 Fold the edges over to lie on the wrong side, and tack down. You will be progging through a double layer of hessian around the edges.

4 Now grid up and transfer your design (see page 29, book 1).

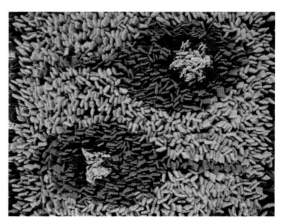

21

**Rug for Evelyn Post**

5 Cut and prepare your fabric tabs. Up to 1" (2½cm) to be wide enough to sit snuggly into the hessian, for durability (see page 22, book one).

6 Using the bodger, begin work through the folded edges, working the outside edge first then fill in your design (see page 10, book two).

7 Once you have worked the whole design, shake out your rug, and snip any uneven ends level on the surface pile.

8 If you want to, stitch a backing on for extra durability.

9 Lay your mat out and wipe you feet on it!

**Bloomsbury Eve Rug**

Fiery English Tile

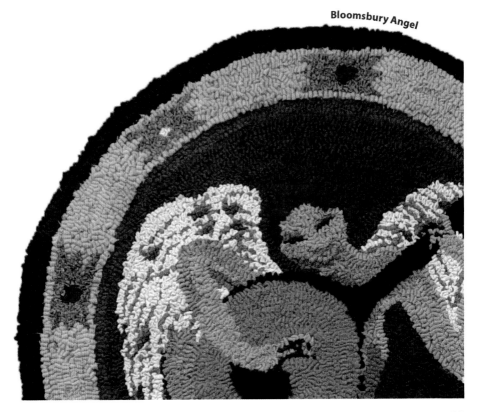

Bloomsbury Angel

23

# Flower Bag
Hooky and Proggy

When making a quick trip to the shops, put your veggies and loaf of bread into this homely and useful bag. It has a tactile looped and clippy surface with a waterproof lining. It will brighten up one of your daily chores, and could also double as a beach bag. I've used different types of fabric in this project to show you how well they work together.

# You will need

- 10oz jute hessian 70" (136cm) square
- Design of your own or the one illustrated
- Recycled textiles
- Old rain mac (for lining)
- Fairly robust cotton fabric for the straps (corduroy, ticking or salecloth) or 1½" cotton tape 30" (77cm) x 3" (8cm) - you'll need two of these
- Rug hook
- Bodger or peg proddy
- Frame (optional)
- Scissors
- Single sheet of newspaper
- Tape measure
- Chalk /old washing up brush/magic marker
- Two or three clothes pegs
- Needle, pins, strong thread
- Sewing machine (optional)
- PVA adhesive

# How to do it

1 Make a 'D' shape newspaper template 14" x 13" (36 x 33cm) and cut it out.

2 Pin this to the hessian and trace around the edge with magic marker – do this twice, one for each side. Leave a 4-5" (10-13cm) gap between each shape to allow for turnings.

**Step 10**

3 Attach hessian to a frame if you are using one, then work the hooked surface, removing from the frame for proggy.

4 Mark out your design within the two 'D' shapes, using first chalk then when you are happy with design, go over with a magic marker.

**Step 12**

5 Cut and prepare your textiles for hooking and proggy (see page 21 book 1).

6 When you have worked both sides, remove from the frame and trim the hessian down to allow for a 2" (5cm) turning.

**Step 16**

26

7 Cut two pieces of hessian the exact size of the 'D' shape template and use adhesive to stick a backing to each of the two sides of your bag.

8 Turn down and stitch the hem onto this backing.

9 Make two straps, by sewing long tubes, and turning them inside out. Alternatively, cut two lengths of carpet tape.

10 Measure in 2" (5cm) from the side edge of your bag and 2" (5cm) from the top. Pin one end of one of the straps in place.

11 Do this with the other end of the strap. Then, using double thread, sew the strap down securely, using a stab running stitch that goes all the way through to the right side. (Bring your needle out between the hooked/proggy surface each time, so the stitches are hidden). Stitch all round the inlaid end of the strap. Repeat for the other strap, on the other side of the bag.

12 To sew the two sides of your bag together - with wrong sides facing, peg the two sides together, then using double thread, oversew the two sides, using fairly close stitches. It doesn't matter if these stitches show, as it will be part of the look of the bag. Leave the top edge as the opening.

13 To create the waterproof lining place the paper template onto wrong side of the rain mac, and trace around the edge. Then, allowing an extra 2" (5cm) for turnings cut out two 'D' shapes.

14 Place them together with right sides facing, and following the template line, pin and stitch, around the two sides and bottom, leaving the top edge open.

15 Place the lining inside your bag, matching up the side seams, and turn in the top edge of the lining, so it meets the top edge of the bag. Pin into place.

16 Stitch the lining to the top edge of your bag, taking care over the straps using a neat oversew stitch. Now its time to go shopping!

# Penny Patch Rug

You can practice your sewing skills by stitching woollen shapes onto a wool blanket backing, using contrasting coloured wool yarn. This charming little mat is a joy to make, and you can recycle old cardigans, wool skirts and scarves along with good old woollen blanket, that you might like to dye. The penny patch mat would also work well as a table runner, as a wall hanging or as a decorative bed cover.

# You will need

- Wool blanket (including a piece big enough to back your rug),
  wool cardigans, wool skirts, other woollen fabrics
  (these fabrics won't fray, so no need for bulky turnings)
- Coloured wool yarn
- Darning/tapestry needle
- Scissors
- 2/3 Sheets of newspaper
- Chalk, ballpoint pen
- Metre stick
- Needles and sewing thread
- Rubberised non-slip mesh (optional)

# How to do it

1 First select your ground woollen fabric and cut to 32" x 22" (81 x 56cm) rounding off the edges.

2 Sew all round the edge using wool yarn and blanket stitch (see page 17 book 2).

3 Cut out several different templates from newspaper, of circles, shingles, and a central oblong.

4 Now choose fabrics to pin your paper templates to. Chalk around them, cut them out, then lay them on the ground material, positioning them carefully.

5 Pin and tack stitch in place.

6 Lay the wool yarn onto the fabrics to find pleasing colourways.

7 Now stitch the shapes to the ground fabric, beginning with the large central oblong shape. Your decorative blanket stitch, over stitch and running stitch will secure the patches in place Do not pull your stitches too tightly, as doing this will distort the work, and you want each piece to lie flat and evenly on the backing material.

8 When you have stitched each piece in place, cut out and sew on the backing.

9 Work two or three lines of long running stitches across the backing, to keep the fabric in place.

10 You could place a non-slip rubberised mesh under your mat if you are using it as a floor mat.

11 Alternatively you could hang your penny patch rug on the wall. If you decide to do this, sew some brass rings to the back to slide a cane through as a hanging device (see page 18 book two).

Cambridge Angel by Jan O'Neill

Oak Leaves and Acorns by Jan O'Neill

Tropical Rug by Lorenzo Gavarini

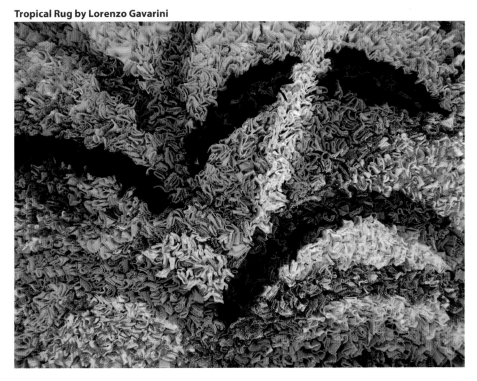

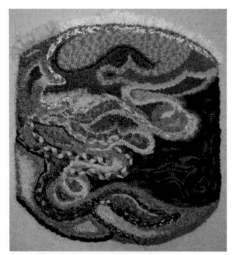

**Water Rug by Lorenzo Gavarini**

**Leaf Rug by Jenni Stuart-Anderson**

**Purple Leaf Rug by Jenni Stuart-Anderson**

**Acorns Bench Runner by Kirsty Post**

**Spiral cushion by Tanya Siniska**

**Kandinsky Mat by Tanya Siniska**

# Listings

**Debbie Siniska**
Glyndale
St Marys Lane
Ticehurst
E.Sussex
TN5 7AX

www.debbiesiniska.co.uk
email: info@debbiesiniska.co.uk
01580 201015

*Rag rugs, workshops, commissions, teaching in schools. rug tools, frames, hessian, greetings cards, felt and beadwork jewellery.*

# Stockists

**Fred Aldous Ltd**
37 Lever Street
Manchester
M1 1LW

www.fredaldous.co.uk
email: sales@fredaldous.co.uk
0161 236 4224

*Rug tools, common and fine hessian*

**Cotswold Woollen Weavers**
Filkins
Lechlade
Gloucestershire
GL7 3JJ

www.cotswoldwoollenweavers.co.uk

email: info@naturalbest.co.uk

*Woven wool sample offcuts in bundles in soft shades – great for rag rug making and braiding.*

- - - - - - -

**Rigby cloth stripping machines**
Route 302, PO box 158
Bridgton
Maine 0409
USA

- - - - - - -

**Whaleys**
Harris Court
Great Horton
Bradford
West Yorkshire
BD7 4EQ

www.whaleys-bradford.ltd.uk
01274 576718

*Fine hessian.*

# Rag Rug Makers

**Louisa Creed**
15 Waterfront House
York, YO23 1PL
www.louisa-creed-ragrugs.co.uk
*Rag rugs & greetings cards*

- - - - - - -

**Heather Ritchie**
Greencroft
Reeth, DL11 6QT
www.rugmaker.co.uk
*Rag rugs, tools and equipment
Heather is the founder of 'Rug Aid' in the
Gambia*

- - - - - - -

**Jenni Stuart-Anderson**
The Birches, Middleton-on-the-Hill
Herefordshire  HR6 0HN
www.jenni.ragrugs.freeuk.com
*Rag rugs, tools and equipment*

# Places of interest

**American Museum in Britain**
Claverton Manor
Bath
BA2 7BD
www.americanmuseum.org

- - - - - - -

**Beamish Museum**
Beamish, Co. Durham
DH9 ORG
www.beamish.org.uk

- - - - - - -

**Charleston Farmhouse**
Charleston,
Firle nr Lewes
E.Sussex
www.charleston.org.uk

**Medieval Hare**

# Pattern Section

Patterns for the following rugs are available to download at a larger scale from www.debbiesiniska.co.uk/oldintonew/patterns

- ✦ Child's Bedside Mat
- ✦ Celebratory Banner
- ✦ Embellished Flotsam Wall Panel
- ✦ Welcome Mat
- ✦ Flower Bag
- ✦ Penny Patch Rug

**Barn Owl Rug**

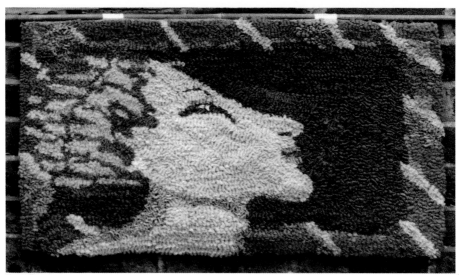

**Face Rug**